The Baby-Sitter's Guide

by Nancy Burgeson

Illustrations by Aija Janums

Troll Associates

Library of Congress Cataloging-in-Publication Data

Burgeson, Nancy.
    The baby-sitter's guide / by Nancy Burgeson.
        p.   cm.—(A Troll survival guide)
    Summary: Provides tips on how to find jobs as a baby sitter and
how to make the experience safe and enjoyable.
    ISBN 0-8167-2467-9 (pbk.)
    1. Babysitting—Handbooks, manuals, etc.—Juvenile literature.
[1. Babysitting.   2. Babysitters.]   I. Title.   II. Series.
HQ769.5.B87 1992
649'.1'0248—dc20   91-14959

Baby-Sitting

Are you thinking about breaking into the baby-sitting business? Does baby-sitting seem like an easy way to make some extra cash? Well, it can be. But it's a big responsibility, too. The best baby sitter is the smart one, and the one who is prepared.

That's what this handbook is all about: Being smart. Being safe. Being prepared. Read it carefully; even bring it along on your baby-sitting jobs. And enjoy the fun world of smart baby-sitting!

But I Have No Experience

So you want to be a baby sitter, but the closest experience you have is watching your best friend's pet gerbil. Well, don't worry! Even *you* can be a world-class baby sitter in no time at all.

How do you prepare to be a baby sitter? If you have younger brothers or sisters, think about what you already know from being around them. If some of your friends are baby sitters, talk with them about their jobs. Your parents can offer advice about what it takes to look after a small child. And in some communities, courses are available. Just remember that, whichever way you choose, it's normal to be nervous about your first baby-sitting assignment. With time and experience, your confidence will grow.

Many, many parents want good, reliable baby sitters. Remember that old phrase "Good help is hard to find"? Well, it's certainly true about finding a baby sitter.

Becoming a baby sitter means becoming a responsible person. Most parents are looking for a sitter for weekend nights. Are you willing to give up your Friday or Saturday nights to hang out with a five-year-old smart aleck? Think about it. Figure out your priorities. Because once you commit yourself, there's no turning back. Someone is depending on you now.

Yes, I Want To Be a Baby Sitter

Okay, so you've made up your mind. Baby-sitting is the right business for you. How do you go about getting that first job? There are lots of ways, really. Look at the list below (and always remember that you *are* in demand):

▶ Ask around. Let people know you're in the market. Perhaps the young mother next door doesn't need a sitter, but her best friend across town just might. This is called networking—spreading the word around to the right people. Do it.

▶ Tell your friends. Do you have friends who baby-sit? Someone may call them for work on a day they're not available. In that case, a friend can recommend you instead. (And don't forget to return the favor!)

▶ Consider advertising. Many baby sitters post their names and phone numbers on bulletin boards in local supermarkets and delis. Some even place ads in the newspaper. Parents looking for baby sitters do, too. Before you go this route, however, think about whether you'd feel comfortable working for total strangers. Discuss it with your parents, as well.

Meeting the Parents

Getting along with parents is just as important as getting along with the kids for whom you are sitting. Don't underestimate your reaction to parents (or their reaction to you). They will be your employers. If you get bad feelings from them, don't take the job. Find someone else to sit for. And if you can, ask others what they think about your prospective employers. Here are some questions to ask yourself when you meet the parents:

▶ Do you like them? This is important. If you do, it will make working for them so much easier.
▶ Do you trust them? If they say they'll be back at 11:30, will they? Use your instincts.

Of course, you might not always have the chance to meet the parents face-to-face before your first assignment. You can still tell a lot about a person on the telephone. Remember, also, that the parents will be interested in knowing more about *you*. Be prepared to give them the phone numbers of other people for whom you've baby-sat, if they ask for references. But check with your other customers first, to be sure it's okay.

The Smart Sitter's Next Step

Once you approve of the parents (and they of you), you can start the serious business of finding out your duties as a baby sitter. Use the questions below as a guide.

► How many children will you be caring for? Remember to get their names and ages. Don't be afraid to turn down an assignment if you think there are more children than you can handle, or if you're hesitant to take care of a nine-month-old infant. The parents will appreciate your honesty.

► What exactly will be your duties? Are you supposed to feed kids, change diapers, bathe them, etc.? This should all be clear to you beforehand.

► When will the parents need your services? Get the exact date and time. Ask for directions to their house if you need them.

► Do they have a pet that will also need to be taken care of? If so, what kind of—and how much—attention does it need?

► Will they provide you with transportation home, or are you expected to make your own arrangements?

What to Charge

The parents are nice, and the kids are okay. And you really don't have anything planned for Saturday night. So you want to take the job, but you don't know how much to charge. What do you do?

► Check around. If any of your friends baby-sit, call them and ask what they charge. It's best to give a competitive price. You don't want to overcharge them or undercharge yourself.

► Take into consideration how many kids you will be sitting for. The more kids, the more you should charge.

► Keep in mind the extent of your duties. If you're expected to prepare dinner, feed the kids, and put them to bed, then by all means, charge more.

► Remember, you're not a housekeeper! If you're expected to do any more than clean up after yourself and the kids, charge more.

Be Prepared!

''A stitch in time saves nine!'' Ever hear that old cliche? Well, it's especially true in the baby-sitting business. If you're a smart sitter (and, of course, you will be), you'll have all the information you need ahead of time. That way, if an emergency occurs, you'll be much less likely to panic.

The following pages contain a fact file of information you should get from the parents *before* they leave the house.

It would be a smart idea to make copies of the form and use them every time you baby-sit.

Smart Sitter's Fact File

Parents' Names _____

Address _____

Telephone Number _____

Kids' Names _____ Age _____

_____ Age _____

_____ Age _____

_____ Age _____

Where Will the Parents Be? _____

Telephone Number _____

What Time Will They Be Home? _____

Nearest Neighbor _____

Address _____

_____

Telephone Number _____

Closest Relative _____

Address _____

_____

Telephone Number _____

Police Department_____

Fire Department_____

Ambulance _____

Family Doctor's Name _____

   Telephone Number _____

Nearest Hospital _____

   Telephone Number _____

Poison Control Center _____

Notes:

_____

_____

_____

_____

_____

_____

_____

_____

_____

_____

Some Last-Minute Details...

Before the parents leave, find out...

► the layout of the house. That way, if something happens to the electricity, at least you'll know your way around.

► your privileges. Can you use the television or VCR? Are you permitted to raid the fridge?

► where the clean diapers are kept. And how the dirty ones are disposed of.

► if you can bring a friend.

► what they want you to do when the phone rings.

► if all the doors are locked.

► the location of the first-aid supplies.

► the bedtimes of the children.

The Moment of Truth

The parents are gone. It's just you and the kids. It's the moment of truth. One kid is staring at you from behind the livingroom couch; the other is in the corner about to cry. What do you do now?

One way to avoid this uncomfortable moment after the parents leave—and to get the kids on your side right away—is to bring along the Smart Sitter's Surprise Box.

The Smart Sitter's Surprise Box

You make up the box yourself. Use an old shoe box or overnight case. Decorate it in bright colors and load it up with surprises the kids will love. Here are some things you could include:

> Rubber ball
> Stuffed animals
> Old books
> Pencils, crayons, and markers
> Paper or coloring books
> A deck of cards
> Clothes pins
> Child-proof scissors

Of course, the kids will probably have most of this stuff themselves, but it will be much more fun and exciting for them to use the toys you brought instead. A word of caution: Make sure you include only safe toys in your surprise box. And don't bring anything that could damage the furniture or create a mess.

The Super Sitter

It's easy to be a super sitter. The main way is to have fun with the kids. So take time and get to know them. They'll behave better, and you'll all have a better time.

The age of the child has a lot to do with the amount and type of attention the child will need. The information below will give you a general idea of what to expect.

Infant

Ages newborn to just before the child is walking. Babies at this age need lots of attention in taking care of their basic needs. They need diapers changed; they need to be fed, clothed, and put to bed.

Toddler

Ages two to four. Ever hear of the Terrible Twos? Well, if you're baby-sitting a toddler, you'll soon find out what it means. Toddlers need lots of attention to keep them out of trouble. Without fail, a toddler will touch something hot, or dangerous, or forbidden. Wear sneakers when you baby-sit a toddler!

Older Children

Ages four and up. Older children tend to play by themselves more than the little ones, but they still need supervision. If there is more than one child and they get along, this job could be a breeze. If there is only one child, you'll probably have to sit down and play with her.

Super Sitting Infants

With the following information, watching an infant can be a fairly simple matter. Without it, you'll spend a lot of wasted time just figuring out where things go and what to do.

Ask the parents the following:
> Where the clean diapers are kept.
> Where the dirty diapers are kept.
> How often you should change the baby.
> How to prepare a bottle.
> How and how often to feed the child.
> If they have any special advice when the baby cries.

Diapers Are Nothing to Be Nervous About

If you've never changed a diaper, it's about time you learned. You can practice at home on a life-size doll. By following these simple steps, diaper changing will be a snap.

1. Place baby on back on bed or on changing table.
2. Grasp baby's ankles.
3. Lift baby's legs and slide clean diaper underneath baby's bottom.
4. Loosen clothing and remove dirty diaper.
5. Put dirty diaper aside. *Never leave baby unattended!*
6. Clean baby's bottom with a washcloth or moist towelette.
7. Sprinkle baby's bottom with powder.
8. Fasten on clean diaper.
9. Put child in safe place (crib or playpen), then dispose of dirty diaper.

Cry Baby!

The baby won't stop crying. What do you do? Check for these common culprits.

► Is the baby too warm or too cold?
► Does the baby's diaper need changing?
► Is the child frightened by something?
► Is there anything sticking the child—a pin, snap, etc.?
► Does the child have a fever?
► Is the baby hungry?

If it's none of these reasons, the child more than likely is missing his parents. The best thing to do is to hold the child in your arms and rock. This will comfort the child, and probably will lull him back to sleep.

Super Sitting Toddlers

Toddlers are always on the go, and so they need your constant attention. They are at the age when they are discovering the world around them and enjoying their newfound mobility.

Safety is the main concern for toddlers, since they tend to get into everything. Always keep toddlers within your eyesight. You'd be amazed at the amount of mischief they can get into in only a few minutes.

Keep toddlers away from stairs, kitchens, bathrooms, and workrooms. These are dangerous places for toddlers, even when they're supervised.

Play! Play! Play! That's the key to keeping a toddler happy. Take out your surprise box. It will really delight children at this age. Let them choose what to play with. Then ask to see their favorite games, toys, and dolls, too.

Watch Out for the Temper Tantrum

It's not unusual for toddlers to experience a classic case of the temper tantrum. The words "you can't make me, you can't make me" may not be totally unfamiliar to you. If you can't find a tangible reason (like being hurt) for why the child is kicking, screaming, crying, and throwing himself on the floor, you can bet it's the temper tantrum.

Leave the child alone for a while. (Of course, keep an ear and eye on the kid just to make sure she's not damaging the house or herself.) The tantrum is usually caused by the child being overtired; it will pass after a little while.

Once the tantrum is over, ask the child to join you in a quiet game or for some milk and cookies. This should be relaxing time, so don't ask the child to play a game of tag.

Super Sitting Older Children

Baby-sitting older children (older than four years, that is) is easier. If there's more than one child, it's easier still. The children will probably entertain themselves with a board game or cards. If there is only one child, you will more than likely have to play along with him.

Older children could also be recruited into helping you watch the younger kids. Make a game out of it. If you're serving dinner, have the eight-year-old play waiter and help serve the food.

While you don't have to watch older children like a hawk, you should always keep an eye on them.

Older children sometimes suffer from temper tantrums, too. See the previous page on how to deal with one.

Three Ways to Cure the Hiccups

1. Have the child hold his breath for a few seconds. Not too long!
2. Have the child take ten sips of water in a row.
3. Have the child breathe slowly and deeply.

(It is not recommended to scare a child in order to get rid of hiccups. The child's better off with the hiccups!)

Injuries

Children are active people, and they always seem to be bumping into things. Ninety-nine per cent of the time, you can handle these minor injuries by yourself—and with little fuss.

Bumps and scratches, nosebleeds, splinters, minor burns, and cuts can be treated by you. Make sure you know where the first-aid supplies are located (usually in the bathroom's medicine cabinet). Wash the wounds or cuts, and cover with a bandage. For minor burns, run cold water over the affected area.

If you feel the slightest bit uncomfortable in treating these minor injuries on your own, call your own parents or a neighbor and ask their advice. If you're still nervous, by all means call the child's parents—it's always better to be safe than sorry. And make sure you let the child's parents know what has happened—no matter how minor—before you leave.

Emergencies

While most of what you have to deal with as a baby sitter will not be an emergency, you should be prepared for one. Remember, the Super Sitter's Fact File you filled out before the parents left (see pages 11-12)? Well, an emergency is the time to use it. Emergencies can be categorized into three types.

An Emergency Where You Should Call the Child's Parents for Advice

Your little charge is complaining of an earache and feels a bit warm. Call the child's parents in situations like this one, and let them decide on a course of action. It might turn out that the child has a chronic earache, and there's nothing you can do. Or it might turn out the child needs medication, which the parents can instruct you on how to administer.

Remember, there is no reason why you should have to decide what to do in these types of situations. Let the parents decide; after all, the child is theirs.

An Emergency Where the Help of an Adult Is Absolutely Necessary

If your charge has fallen and is bleeding uncontrollably, call whoever can help you the fastest—your parents, the child's doctor, the next-door neighbor. Once the situation is under control, call the child's parents and let them now what's happened.

This would include any situation where the child's life might be threatened. In this situation, call 911 or an ambulance immediately. Give your name and your employer's address, and explain the problem as clearly as you can. Wait on the phone in case there are instructions for you to follow. Call the child's parents as soon as it's possible to let them know the situation.

If the child swallows some poisonous substance, call the poison control center and ask their advice. Sometimes vomiting should be induced in the child, sometimes not, depending on the poison. The poison control center will guide you.

There are two medical emergencies that need your instant action. In these cases, you can't wait for outside help.

Choking

Infant: For babies under a year, turn child on her stomach on your lap with her head down and your hand under her neck. Hit the child between the shoulder blades four times. Check the child's mouth for the object blocking the passage. If it has not come out, repeat procedure.

Toddler or Older Child: Lie child on his back, or put child in sitting or standing position. Place one hand on the stomach just under the rib cage, and administer a sharp upward thrust. Repeat several times if necessary. You can also stand *behind* the child, with one fist just under his rib cage, thumb inward. Put your other hand over the fist and quickly push upward.

Mouth-to-Mouth Resuscitation

Many first-aid and lifesaving classes teach this technique. Taking one of these courses will show you exactly what to do. If a child stops breathing, no oxygen reaches the brain. Brain damage can occur in minutes. A class will show you how to turn the child on his back and breathe gentle shallow breaths into his mouth. There are also books on the subject. It's a technique worth learning for any situation.

Bedtime Blues

You never met a kid that wanted to go to bed, right? Well, bedtime is never going to be the easiest thing a sitter has to deal with. But neither does it have to be the worst thing. When bedtime comes around, remain calm and patient!

Infants are usually the easiest to put to bed. A clean diaper and a full bottle should do nicely. A little rocking and humming might be all the encouragement the little one needs. Just follow the child's usual procedure.

It gets a bit more difficult with older children. It's probably a good idea to warn the children ahead of time that bedtime is approaching. Give them some time to adjust to the idea.

Often a bedtime snack eases the procedure, as does a bedtime story. If the child is frightened about going to bed, reassure and comfort her that you'll be nearby should she need you. Also, you can leave on a light or open the door a bit.

And if the child is still too overexcited to go to bed, let her lie in bed with a book or a favorite stuffed toy. She'll be asleep before you know it.

Some Safety Tips for You

► Make sure all doors are locked and all windows are closed.

► If you hear a suspicious noise, call the police.

► If the child's parents come home drunk and are supposed to drive you home, call your parents. Never get in a car with someone who has had too much to drink.

► If the child's parents do anything that makes you feel uncomfortable, tell your parents.

► If the child's parents aren't home when they're supposed to be, call your parents and tell them you'll be late. If they're really late, and your mother says you have to come home, call them at the place they're supposed to be and tell them your parents want you home soon.

► Do not open the door for anyone.

Repeat Customers

So it's gone well? If it seems likely you'll be called back for more work in the future (and if you're looking forward to it!), by all means don't throw out the Fact File you filled out on pages 11-12. It will save you and your customers a great deal of time if you have their basic information on hand whenever you are needed. It will also show that you are responsible, organized, and dedicated to what you are doing.

Establish a system for keeping this information on file. There's no need to waste time on each assignment getting the names and numbers of neighbors, relatives, and other emergency contacts again and again. The following Client Update Sheet will give you all the information you need for any new baby-sitting assignment once you've worked for someone before. Copy it and bring it with your Fact File sheets each time you report to work.

It helps to fill out the top half of the form immediately after your first assignment, while your memories are still fresh. Then, if some time passes before the parents call you again, you won't have to relearn all the things you learned about the family the first time!

Client Update Sheet

Notes from Previous Assignment
(Do the children have any special likes or dislikes?
Allergies? Food restrictions? Television rules?
Favorite books or games? Write these down while
you remember—and ask each time if they've
changed.)

Next appointment:

Date _____

Time _____

Address _____

Where Will the Parents Be? _____

Telephone Number_____

What Time Will They Be Home?_____

Any Special Instructions for Tonight?

The Smart Sitter's Sendoff

If you keep in mind the simple tips and guidelines you have just read, baby-sitting will be a rewarding business for you.

And here's one final tip: A smart sitter has a level head, clever ideas, and patience. A smart sitter is you!